LEVEL
2

D0979343

Bees

Laura Marsh

Washington, D.C.

For Tracy, friend, educator, and beekeeper —L. F. M.

Trade paperback ISBN: 978-1-4263-2281-5
Reinforced library binding ISBN: 978-1-4263-2282-2

Editor: Shelby Alinsky
Art Director: Amanda Larsen
Editorial: Snapdragon Books
Designer: YAY! Design
Photo Editor: Christina Ascani
Special Projects Assistant: Kathryn Williams
Rights Clearance Specialists: Michael Cassady & Mari Robinson
Manufacturing Manager: Rachel Faulise
Production Editor: Mike O'Connor
Managing Editor: Grace Hill

The publisher and author gratefully acknowledge the expert content review of this book by Marla Spivak, PhD, MacArthur Fellow and Distinguished McKnight Professor in Entomology, University of Minnesota, and the literacy review of this book by Mariam Jean Dreher, professor of reading education, University of Maryland, College Park.

Honeybees are in trouble, and bee colonies are collapsing. Scientists think the use of pesticides, mite infestation, diseases, and, mostly, loss of flowering habitat are major factors. To learn more and also find out ways to help bees, ask a parent to visit thehoneybeeconservancy.org.

Photo Credits
Cover, Michael Durham/Minden Pictures; 1, l i g h t p o e t/Shutterstock; 3 (ALL), Vinicius Tupinamba/Shutterstock; 4-5, szefei/Shutterstock; 6 (CTR LE), sauletas/Shutterstock; 6 (LO), Dionisvera/Shutterstock; 6 (CTR RT), HLPhoto/Shutterstock; 7 (UP), Tinydevil/Shutterstock; 7 (LO), Aleksey Troshin/Shutterstock; 8 (LO), Darlyne A. Murawski/National Geographic Creative; 9, Brian Stablyk/Getty Images; 10 (LE), Paul Starosta/Corbis; 10 (CTR), Heidi & Hans-Juergen Koch/Corbis; 11 (UP), Ariel Bravy/Shutterstock; 12 (UP), alslutsky/Shutterstock; 12 (CTR RT), Werner Forman/Universal Images Group/Getty Images; 12 (LOLE), Maxal Tamor/Shutterstock; 13 (UPRT), djgis/Shutterstock; 13 (CTR LE), Redmond Durrell/Alamy; 13 (CTR RT), John Burke/Getty Images; 13 (LOLE), Vorobyeva/Shutterstock; 14, Pairoj Sroyngern/Shutterstock; 15, Yuri Kravchenko/Alamy; 16, Ed Phillips/Shutterstock; 18-19 (RT), taraki/Shutterstock; 19 (CTR), Harry Rogers/Science Source; 20, Cordelia Molloy/Science Source; 21 (UPLE), Eduardo Ramirez Sanchez/Shutterstock; 21 (CTR), Andrey_Kuzmin/Shutterstock; 22 (UPLE), Paul Starosta/Corbis; 22-23 (UP), NinaHenry/iStock.com; 23 (UPRT), Eric Tourneret/Visuals Unlimited/Corbis; 23 (LO), LSkywalker/Shutterstock; 24-25, Steve Hopkin/Getty Images; 26-27, Solvin Zankl/Nature Picture Library; 28 (CTR), Christian Kober/Getty Images; 29, Vinicius Tupinamba/Shutterstock; 30 (UPRT), George D. Lepp/Science Source; 30 (CTR LE), Darlyne A. Murawski/National Geographic Creative; 30 (LOLE), taraki/Shutterstock; 30 (LORT), Ed Phillips/Shutterstock; 31 (UPLE), Nikola Spasenoski/Shutterstock; 31 (CTR RT), Karl Gehring/The Denver Post/Getty Images; 31 (CTR LE), Arne Dedert/dpa/Corbis; 31 (LORT), Uwe Anspach/Corbis; 32 (UPLE), Harry Rogers/Science Source; 32 (UPRT), StudioSmart/Shutterstock; 32 (CTR LE), Jimmy phu Huynh/Shutterstock; 32 (CTR RT), MMCez/Shutterstock; 32 (LOLE), Howard Sandler/Shutterstock; 32 (LORT), Bernard Castelein/Nature Picture Library; header (THROUGHOUT), Ramona Kaulitzki/Shutterstock; vocab (THROUGHOUT), elenka_a/Shutterstock

National Geographic supports K–12 educators with ELA Common Core Resources.
Visit natgeoed.org/commoncore for more information.

Table of Contents

Buzzzz!

Outside the sun is shining.
The flowers are blooming.
And the bees
are buzzing.

When some people see bees, they run. Others might not notice the bees. But let's stop and take a closer look. Bees are helpful. Our world needs bees!

Helpful Bees

Bees help both people and plants. Honeybees make honey and beeswax. People use these things in lots of ways.

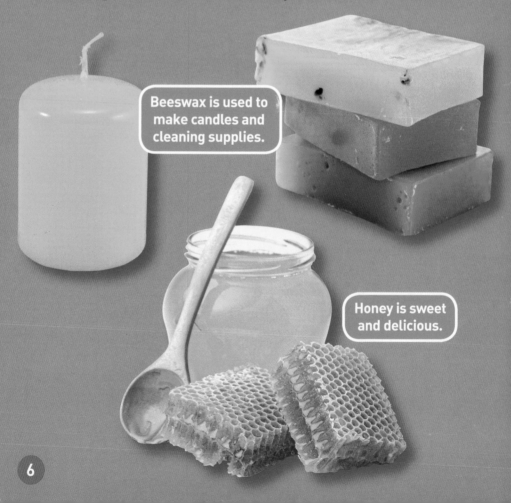

Beeswax is used to make candles and cleaning supplies.

Honey is sweet and delicious.

A bee sits on the flower of a strawberry plant.

All kinds of bees help plants make seeds. Seeds can grow into new plants. Some of those plants give us fruits and vegetables. We can thank bees for strawberries, apples, almonds, tomatoes, and many other foods.

Pollen Power

When a bee lands on a flower, the flower's pollen rubs off on the bee. Pollen sticks to tiny hairs on the bee's body.

Buzz Word

POLLEN: A sticky, yellow powder made by flowers

This bee has pollen all over its body.

When the bee travels to another flower, pollen from the bee brushes off onto the new flower. This is called pollination (pol-uh-NAY-shun). Now the new flower can start to make seeds.

A bee's leg has special hairs that form a basket. The bee brushes pollen into the basket. Then it flies back to the nest. This pollen is used as food for baby bees.

These pollen baskets are filled with pollen. Only female bees have them.

empty pollen basket

tongue on a bumblebee

Bees collect nectar from flowers too. They drink nectar with their tongues. Some bees make honey out of nectar. These bees are called honeybees.

Buzz Word

NECTAR: A sweet, sugary juice that flowers make

7 COOL FACTS
About Bees

1 The garden bumblebee has a tongue that is as long as its body.

Humans collected honey from bees as early as 6000 B.C. **2**

3

Bees have four wings—two large wings and two small wings.

Bees can see colors. They are most likely to land on flowers that are blue, purple, or yellow.

4

5

Farmers often hire beekeepers to bring bees to their fields. The bees pollinate the farmers' crops.

Honeybees do a dance called "the waggle." Scientists think that the dance shows other bees in the hive where the best nectar is.

6

7

About one-third of the food on our planet grows because of bees' pollination.

A Bee or Not a Bee?

It's easy to mistake other insects for bees. They often look alike.

Bee

Has hair all over its body that helps catch pollen

Eats nectar and pollen from flowers

Has pollen baskets, if the bee is female

But there are ways to tell them apart. Take a closer look at a bee and a yellow jacket wasp, which is not a bee. Do you see what's different?

Yellow Jacket Wasp

Does not have much hair

Eats mostly meat, such as other insects

Does not have pollen baskets

A World of Bees

Most bees are solitary bees.

About 20,000 kinds of bees live on Earth. All bees are either solitary (SOL-uh-ter-ee) bees or social (SOH-shul) bees.

A solitary bee makes a nest for its young. The nest is inside a hole in the ground, in wood, in walls, or in plant stems. Solitary bees collect pollen. But they do not make honey or beeswax.

Buzz Words

SOLITARY BEES: Bees that live alone

SOCIAL BEES: Bees that live in a group

Social bees live with many other bees. A group of social bees is called a colony (KOL-uh-nee). A colony of bees lives in a hive.

Honeybees are one kind of social bee. As many as 50,000 honeybees may live in one hive. Bees care for their young there. They make and store honey in the hive too.

Buzz Word

HIVE: An open space within a tree, structure, or box where social bees live together

honeybee hive

Home Sweet Home

Inside the hive, honeybees build with beeswax. The bees mold the wax into six-sided shapes called cells. Lots of cells together make a honeycomb.

Buzz Word

HONEYCOMB: A sheet of six-sided cells made of beeswax

The bees put nectar from flowers into some of the cells. As the nectar gets thicker, it turns into honey. Bees eat the honey for food.

Each cell has one egg.

Adult bees feed and care for the young.

Other cells in the hive hold bee eggs. There is one egg in each cell. The eggs hatch. The young bees grow and change. After 21 to 24 days, the young bees become adults.

These young are almost ready to come out of the cells.

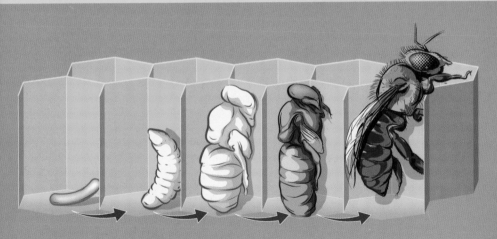

A bee starts as an egg and becomes an adult in about three weeks.

Busy as a Bee

Every honeybee in the colony has a special job. These jobs keep the colony healthy and strong.

There is only one queen bee. She is bigger than the other bees. She lays all of the eggs—up to 1,500 per day!

Worker bees surround the queen. She is the largest bee in the middle.

There are two other kinds
of bees in the colony.

This worker bee is
collecting pollen.

Drone bees are male bees. Their job is to help the queen make eggs.

Worker bees have many jobs. These females feed the queen and care for the young. They build the hive and make honey. On long flying trips, they collect pollen and nectar. They also guard the hive against enemies. Whew, that's a lot of work!

Keeping Bees

Beekeepers wear special clothes to protect them from stings.

Some humans build honeybee hives out of wooden boxes. Beekeepers take care of the hives and collect the honey.

Beekeepers also check the bee colonies to make sure they are healthy. Beekeepers know how important bees are to our world.

Bee Aware

Here are some tips for staying safe around bees:

- Move slowly. Don't wave your arms or jump around. If a bee thinks it's being attacked, it may sting.

- If a bee comes near you, stand still or walk slowly away.

- Do not swat at a bee. Let it fly away on its own.

- Do not disturb any bee nest or honeybee hive. The bees will defend their home and may sting an attacker.

- If you are stung by a bee, put ice on the sting.

- If you leave bees alone, they will probably leave you alone.

QUIZ WHIZ

How much do you know about bees? After reading this book, probably a lot. Take this quiz and find out.

Answers are at the bottom of page 31.

1

What do honeybees do in a hive?

A. live with other honeybees
B. raise their young
C. make and store honey
D. all of the above

2

What is pollen?

A. a kind of bee
B. a powder made by flowers
C. a kind of plant
D. a place where bees live

Social bees live _____.

A. with other bees
B. alone
C. with ants
D. with wasps

3

4

Bees are helpful because they
_____.

A. make honey
B. help plants make seeds
C. make beeswax
D. all of the above

There is only one of these in a bee colony.

A. a drone
B. a worker
C. a queen
D. a cell

5

6

What's the name of the honeybee's dance?

A. the waggle
B. the hustle
C. the wiggle
D. the chicken

What does a bee do with its long tongue?

A. brushes pollen into baskets
B. drinks nectar
C. attracts the queen
D. sticks it out at other bees

7

HIVE: An open space within a tree, structure, or box where social bees live together

HONEYCOMB: A sheet of six-sided cells made of beeswax

NECTAR: A sweet, sugary juice that flowers make

POLLEN: A sticky, yellow powder made by flowers

SOCIAL BEES: Bees that live in a group

SOLITARY BEES: Bees that live alone